BURST FORTH ...ARISE

BURST FORTH ...ARISE

How to be Free to Live your Dream,

Fulfil Your Purpose and Succeed

ANDREA RICHARDS

PALMER PUBLISHING HOUSE

All stories related in this book are true, but most of the names have been changed to protect the privacy of the people mentioned.

ISBN: 978-976-96886-1-2 (Paperback)
ISBN: 978-976-96886-0-5 (Hardcover)
ISBN: 978-976-96886-3-6 (Kindle)
ISBN: 978-96886-2-9 (eBook)

Published by
PALMER PUBLSHING HOUSE
Moneague PO., St. Ann,
Jamaica. W.I.
Email: Richards.andrea10@yahoo.com

DEDICATION

To the memory of my grandmother

JOSEPHINE SAVERY

who always supported my desire to excel and
never held back her best.

To my mother

BEVERLY BRISCOE

The warrior who demonstrated grit and
the difference strong mindset can make.

ACKNOWLEDGMENTS

All glory, honour and praise be to my Lord and Saviour, Jesus Christ, the Author of creation. Thank you for providing all guidance and help to make this dream possible.

Special thanks to my supportive husband, Lloyd, who after reading the draft, expressed confidence that it will make a difference in the lives of others. Your words of affirmation fueled the realization of the vision.

Sincere thanks to my children, Melek and Khara who conveyed much excitement and words of support during the process.

I must also thank Marcia Thomas and Covell Hall-Golding, my colleagues, and friends, who willingly provide valuable feedback

To C. Ruth Taylor who leads the Indie Authorpreneur Team, through whom I have garnered essential information on the publishing process, I express a big thank you.

Sincere thanks, Denise Harty, your interest has really served to cheer me forward to live out this aspect of my purpose.

CONTENTS

Then your light will break forth like the dawn, and your healing will quickly appear; then your righteousness will go before you, and the glory of the Lord will be your rear guard.

Isaiah 58:8

Introduction

We were created with the capacity to succeed and overcome. We are designed for greatness, which means that greatness is embedded in our DNA. However, many have not moved from what I term the "Aspiration Station." If you are still in the fight to overcome some issues and to reach your destiny, then this book is for you.

Burst Forth…Arise was written to inspire, motivate, transform, and activate the "stalled and the stuck" to burst forth and arise! It is never easy to move from where you are stuck and get going, but it's possible with God. People are in the habit of believing that they can make it without God, but you will only feel a sense of success and never have a true feeling of satisfaction. There will always be the feeling of missing out or not achieving enough. *Burst Forth…Arise: How to be Free to Live your Dream, Fulfill Your Purpose and Succeed,* will inspire you to keep going with a sense of satisfaction. The Word of God demonstrates that it is possible to have peace during a storm. This was achieved because Jesus was present on the boat. He has the power to do all things.

There are so many lids placed upon us by ourselves, our families, friends, communities, and society, that we always seem to be playing catch up. During the reading of this book, it is hoped you will burst forth and arise, throwing off all the lids and rising to walk into our God-ordained purpose. We must understand that a prophetic word spoken over us does not mean it is going to happen. We must take hold of the call placed on us.

When Christ encountered the paralyzed, he would inquire about their desire. Then he would instruct the person to participate in their deliverance. "Arise and take up your mat and walk" (John 5:8). In other words, for the fulfilment of the word to take effect we must do our part.

Each person was born for a purpose, no matter the circumstances behind their conception, as there are no mistakes. It is not even confined to your childhood experiences, family background, or economic status. We were designed for a purpose. Various things trap us from fulfilling our assignment on this earth. This book is written to help you figure out that purpose and to get you to understand how to walk into your divine appointment. There are several ways to break the cocoon that holds you bound, and these will be shared so you can burst forth!

The prophet Isaiah wrote, "Then your light will burst forth like the morning, your new skin will quickly grow over your wound; your righteousness will precede you, and Adonai's glory will follow you" (Isaiah 58:8). For centuries, human beings have been on a quest to answer the questions of purpose and destiny. The time assigned to many has run out and they have never found out the reason for their existence or if they have fulfilled their true purpose.

There is an intrinsic urge within to find our purpose and fulfil our destiny. It is how we were designed by the Creator of heaven and earth, with a sense of purpose. The creation story in the book of Genesis explains clearly that God created human beings in His image and likeness. This means the God who has a purpose behind His design has placed within us that same sense of purpose. Therefore, experiences, both negative and positive, have a purpose in our lives, "for all things work together for the good of those who love Him and are called according to His purpose."

Many have tried to find out by consulting mediums, spirits, horoscopes, and others looking for a word from God through prophets and apostles. Life experiences have further compounded the problem, causing persons to spiral into confusion and exploration of various deeds, jobs, ministries, and partners.

There is just a sense in your heart that this cannot be it; this is not it; there is more to my life, and I need to walk into it. It is with this similar sense of duty (purpose) that I undertook this process of writing. I have always felt a sense that I should write books as a part of my purpose, but I have delayed for lack of knowledge about the process and fear of failure. It is my inward desire to write to inspire and help others overcome the obstacles life throws at them. Therefore, this book has become a reality.

Paul, the Apostle wrote, "Not that I have already obtained all this, or have already arrived at my goal, but I am pressing on to take hold of that for which Christ Jesus took hold of me" (Philippians 3:12). These words express my exact feelings. This book is my effort to fulfil a part of the high calling of God upon my life. I know you will be helped by this book penned from my heart as I felt led by the Lord, and I believe with this, I would have walked into a part of my purpose. There will be more books written as I sense it in my spirit that I have not arrived at my goal but it in partial fulfilment mode. Whatever you sense God has called you to but have not been able to arise and take hold of it is time to step up, Burst Forth…Arise. Time is too short to laze about fiddling our thumbs hoping one day it will happen. It is not even enough to pray, as God expects us to participate and move into that which He has placed in us to do. I am convinced that this is the place to begin.

1

Purpose Behind the Design

An architect is given the task of conceptualizing an idea presented by a client or from his own mind. It is never at the end of the design that the architect decides where or what will become of it or the use of it. There is usually a need that is seen that triggers the idea of designing something that could address the issue. In other words, the designer uses a premise to create the design. So too, the Master Builder. When God saw nothingness and void, He created the earth, and after that, He created man to take care of it. Simply put, God created and further created to make man have dominion over all living things. Before we were born, God already decided His purpose for our lives, so there are no accidents births, even if our mothers and fathers did not plan on having us.

Some people are trapped by the words of their parents, or other important figures in their lives, who tell them they are making mistakes, so they never reach their full potential. If this describes you, I want to let you know that this does not have to be your fate. You have the power to break the chains, pry open the bar, destroy the ceiling, and be free. I also want to dispel that lie today, for with God there are no coincidences or accidents. He intended for you to be here at this time, with that family, in this country, and for a specific reason. You are not a design flaw or mistake. You measure up and you matter. Therefore, if you are feeling lost, or like a victim, unproductive, lacking confidence, or unworthy, know that God thought of you prior to your existence.

According to the initial design, Adam and Eve were created to be stewards who are in a relationship with God and man. In the New Testament, after the act of redemption done by Jesus so all men could be saved, an additional purpose was placed on human beings, that is, that of a witness. Whether the assignment is accepted or not, there is purpose on our lives. If we do not take up the mandate, then we begin to feel a sense of dissatisfaction and distress.

Life is like a puzzle; it is about identifying the pieces, then accepting what we were designed for, and being deliberate in walking in our purpose, so it will all come together. The wrong piece in the wrong place distorts the real image, but when the pieces fall into place, the beauty of the picture becomes evident. A lost piece of the puzzle makes the puzzle useless; in the same way if persons neglect to find and walk into our purpose. Like the Pharisees and experts in the law, you can reject the purpose for which you were created (St. Luke 7:30), but it is not a wise decision because the cost is too great.

Designed to be a Leader

When God decided to create mankind, He had a clear purpose in mind. In the book of Genesis, during the greatest design plan ever completed, God created man. He knew this wonderful world needed to be maintained. In Genesis 2:15-19, God reveals the purpose behind His design. Adam was to "work it and take care of it" and to name the living things God created. Adam was obviously assigned the role of manager or steward over creation.

Human beings have a spiritual responsibility to take care of the environment. Therefore, cleaning, planting, caring for living things, and caring about the impact of one's actions on others is necessary. The only way people get greater responsibilities is after they have demonstrated care for the small things or tasks. This means that if you are desirous of owning something, you should not just desire it but give attention to what you presently own or that which is under your care. It also includes doing your best in your current position at work so that you can be considered for greater things.

According to Luke 12:48, "To whom much is given, much is required." This is not limited to material things but includes time and knowledge. If knowledge gained is not used, you lose it. During my sixth form at high school in Jamaica, I was taught the skill of writing in Shorthand, which I grasped very well. I received a distinction for it at the Caribbean Secondary Examination level. However, I have not been placed in situations that require the skill, so I am now ignorant of it. My documents say I can, but I cannot. Hence, my statement, whatever we do not use, we lose. Let us push towards the meaningful use of our time, resources, and skills.

As stewards, working for God Almighty must be our top priority. At work, we must give our best by spending quality time fulfilling tasks undertaken and even volunteering to start or lead an initiative. However, we still should set aside time to do the work of the Lord.

Do not agree to lead a ministry and then give little time to planning, executing or praying. Time with God should not be given as a last resort; rather, it should be included when we allocate our time. Too many people, instead of using what time they have been given to fulfil their purpose or to build up others and the kingdom of God, give their best to secular society only.

The story of the talent, found in Matthew 25:14-30, is a warning which should be adhered to. No one should expect to get more responsibility if they neglect that which they have already been assigned. Burying your talent results in downsizing. Others will step in and walk through your open door because you were unprepared to handle it. In the story, those who used what they had been given, received more responsibilities. However, the one who abdicated the job given, lost that which was given. It is important for us then, to determine the results we want, which will determine the action to be taken.

If we want to accomplish much in life and be successful, care should be taken to ensure what we are gifted or consent to do gets done at the agreed time and at the highest quality. "Allow no sleep to your eyes…go to the ant, you sluggard; consider its ways and be wise!" (Proverbs 6:4). This is a philosophy to be adopted for life. The verse instructs us to examine the ant as they toil and learn how to achieve. A close look at them will reveal that in order to achieve greatness it is not an overnight accomplishment but requires systematic, deliberate and non-stop steps to get it done. It means success comes from consistent, timeless toiling, which involves collaborating with others.

Keeping ones' goal at the forefront of the mind will keep them on task. When others are distracted by pleasure and rest, you should be engaged in making things happen. This is your opportunity to change, to assume your God-intended role, to learn to utilize your skills, to make better choices, and to organize your life so you walk in purpose.

Designed to Connect

In the story of man's creation, God would meet with Adam and Eve each evening for fellowship, indicating that they had become His companions. While God had other beings around, He took the time to meet with His creation daily. This shows human beings are also designed to have fellowship with God. He intended this to be a way of life, where we meet with Him without failing. Meeting with God would aid in revealing His true nature and will.

Clearly, relationships were His intention. Even after Adam and Eve sinned, He still made attempts to connect with humanity, from Cain and Abel to Abraham, through the prophets, and to Saul on the Damascus Road. It is about setting aside an agreed time and sticking to it.

God still wants that meeting time, which would help to shed light on the dark areas of our lives.

He is the Light who dispels darkness, so where we are unclear of His purpose, meeting with Him would bring fresh revelation, causing us to strive and walk in confidence. This explains the reason man is always seeking to make something lord, that is, seeking some higher power for directives.

Many things have been used to replace God, including idolizing others, for example, superstars, self, or objects, and groups, because we were created to have relationships. When this aspect of the relationship is given to the wrong source, human beings find themselves in trouble. We experience a sense of disillusionment, disconnect, distress which leads to despair.

God is bent on having a relationship with us, so He gave His only Son to restore that which was broken revealed in the prayer recorded in John 17:3. There were reasons behind the design of the first man and woman;

it is safe to deduce that there is a reason for the rest of humanity. God demonstrated to us the importance of forgiveness for progress to be made and purpose to be accomplished. He gave up His only Son to pay for our sins and free us to serve Him. Unforgiveness can hinder our purpose. Instead of focusing on our calling and developing our potential, one's mind is engaged in feelings of hurt over and over. It must be dealt with for progress to be made. Firstly, if we 'harbor iniquity in our hearts, the Lord will not hear us' (Psalm 16:18). Our prayers are blocked from God's ears if we harbor sin, under which unforgiveness is classified.

The desire for relationship is not limited to God but to others. "The Lord God said, it is not good for the man to be alone. I will make a helper suitable for him" in Genesis 2:18. There is a misconception that we do not need others. We can survive on our own, but this view is not supported by scripture. While we cannot take everyone along on the journey, as they may sabotage our destiny, we need others. Some will serve as motivators, others as mentors, and still others as destiny helpers who will use their resources (human and otherwise) to connect us with the right people or opportunities.

David needed Goliath for others to recognize the anointing on his life. Joshua required Moses to affirm his appointment to lead, and Mary required Elizabeth to prophesy, confirming the assignment placed on her life. You need to find that person who is ahead of you in ministry, on the job, and at the level you want to be and allow them to speak about and model success. Speaking success entails sharing the lessons they have learned along the way, providing a network, and guiding you through the process. Doing it alone is possible but will be more difficult and could limit the level at which you will operate.

Choose carefully who you spend time with to ensure that it is not wasted time and that the relationship grows stronger. Who we associate with can determine how successful we are in life? Therefore, having the right influencers is key.

We carry around a deep desire to find a purpose for life and to become successful, which comes from the design of the Master Builder. God has predestined us according to His plans (Ephesians 1:11). Each person is handpicked by God to be present to fulfill His plans. No one was born by accident, no matter the circumstances under which they were conceived. It means; therefore, something must be done to ensure we find our purpose and accomplish what we were created to do. It conveys the message that God expects us to walk into our purpose to carry out His plans. Ephesians 2:10 states "For we are God's handiwork, created in Christ Jesus to do good works, which God prepared in advance for us to do...". The scripture makes it clear that we were created by God who has already prepared what we are to do. It makes sense to ask Him.

Designed to be a Witness

The final words of a person in most culture is honoured by those left behind. In Matthew 28:18-20, as Jesus prepared to ascend to his Father, He charged the believers to be witnesses, specifically to share the Gospel so that others might come to know Him.

Paul, the Apostle demonstrated a level of determination to fulfil this command. Though in chains, he continued to share his conversion experience so other may turn from their ways. At one point appearing before King Agrippa, Paul endeavored share the message of salvation by telling his story, forcing King Agrippa to ask him if he thought in this short time, he could convert him to Christianity. Paul answered in the affirmative. So, as we burst forth, the mandate given must be held in high regard, be a witness.

Sharing how our lives have been changed is such a powerful statement that it should never be underestimated. You do not have to be concerned that you do not have a Paul conversion story. Just share yours. I remember when that reality hit me. You see, I grew up going to church. It was my neighbour, Fay Hall, being a witness, who took me with her and later my other siblings. I decided to accept

Jesus Christ as my Saviour towards the end of a children's church session, so I had no drama. I would not share my testimony because it was so simple, or so I thought. But it dawned on me after an evangelism training video that there are others just like me in church, probably thinking they are saved. They may take it for granted that they do not need to make a commitment to follow Jesus because of their frequent attendance at church. If they are under such deceptive thinking, my testimony could make the difference in their lives. It could enable them to recognize the limitation or deception in their thoughts and take the necessary steps to commit their lives to Jesus Christ. I now share my own story, for what it is worth.

Being a witness does not mean talking about another person's experience but sharing what you have seen or heard. People can tell if you have had an encounter with God, so do not embellish the story. Just share it without reservation. The more you tell your salvation story, the better it will come together and the more impactful it will be. Those who do struggle to believe in Jesus as Lord could be drawn to Him through your experience.

If you have not made a personal commitment to follow Jesus, it is quite easy. All that is required is an acknowledgement of His Lordship, a confession of sins committed, and a pledge to follow Him. After this, you become adopted into the family of Jesus Christ. Find a Bible-believing church to attend and seal your commitment with baptism. The emptiness you are experiencing will leave, and you will feel a sense of joy and purpose.

When a manufacturer designs a product, there is a purpose behind each item produced. Many times, we do not use all the features, missing out on the full value of the product. Let us not be that product that is underutilized because we do not operate based on design.

No matter what we have been told about our abilities or appearance, know this: we are created for a purpose and until we walk into that, there will always be a sense of loss inside.

My Journal: Points to Remember

Do you accept the reason behind your design? How will you seek to modify your present reality to ensure you walk in purpose as a leader, to have a relationship with God or live as a witness? What is your take-away?

2

Finding My Purpose

There is a purpose to your life. Hopefully, you have accepted that fact. God did not make a mistake in your birth. He has created you to do great things which He has prepared in advance for you. When I asked myself the age-old question, "What's my purpose?", it took some time and much reflection for me to understand. Your purpose is already established; therefore, you do not have to make it up.

There is no real formula, but what I learned along the way is what I want to share with you. It is never too late to walk into your purpose!

Pray for Direction

"Ask, and you shall receive, that your joy may be full," (John 16:24). This is a promise, and all promises are signed by God, for He has put His word above His very name. His signature is attached to His words. Then, Jesus instructs us to ask Him for what we need, and then assures us that what we have asked for will be granted. When we are unsure of our purpose, we tend to be unsettled and disturbed, which robs us of our peace. For joy to be ours, it requires us to ask God for guidance and revelation about His purpose for our lives.

If you have questions about a piece of equipment you purchased, the person to give you the best information about it would be the manufacturer. That person can reveal how much power is built in, the types of parts used, and the capabilities of the machine. In the same way, God, being the Creator, whether we believe it or not, is the only one who has the master plan for us, His creation. Sending up a request is necessary for the download from heaven to be deposited.

It took a long time in prayer for me to hear what God wanted me to do. I am still listening for His direction as it is not a one-off download but continuous revelation.

Many people have been trying an "easier route", going to a prophet or an obeah worker, or astrologer, who are limited in their ability to see your end from your beginning. God genuinely wants us to ask Him questions. He encourages us to seek Him and promises that we will find Him if we seek Him with all our hearts (Jeremiah 29:13). When God reveals our purpose, we can then ask Him to use us in the capacity for which we were built. If where you are today, in relation to occupation, relationships, ministry, financial status, or mindset, you are not feeling a sense of fulfilment but more out of place, you are probably out of purpose and success will be a fleeting thought or a dream.

Jabez prayed, "Oh, that You would bless me indeed, and enlarge my territory, that Your hand would be with me, and that You would keep me from evil, that I may not cause pain!" (1 Chronicles 4:10). His request was a sign that He believed God could. In asking, it conveys the message that God is my source. It says you know He can be trusted. Jabez's request for his territory to be expanded, can be interpreted to mean, widening the scope of my influence, so I can be used in supernatural ways. I believe the prayer of Jabez is a model showing us how to pray as we seek to discover our purpose.

We were created to do great work, and many have ended their lives without fulfilling it. Do not make that your testimony. When you come to your latter years, it brings much peace when you can say, I was able to be a blessing to others as was designed. The blueprint needs to be revealed, and the how is also necessary, and it will take seeking the heart of God for you to know what that is. I am determined to do what I can in the time I am allotted, to achieve success as I walk in purpose. It is my intention to live and die with no regret; you should as well.

There are many examples in the Bible when the kings faced serious decisions that they went before the Lord or asked the priest to consult God. Inevitably, once they were obedient to the guidance provided, they were successful. Sometimes they did not have to do much, for He fought for them. They were only required to stand or position themselves by faith, and God helped them overcome. Finding your purpose is not something to take lightly, or to disregard; it should be done with much time spent in the presence of God listening.

Conduct Role Explorations

As I began by praying about my purpose, each morning before attending church, I told the Lord that I was open to Him using me in any way. On those Sundays I was always asked to participate in the service and my response was always yes, no matter how uncomfortable I felt about the task. He had me reading the scripture, collecting offerings, dusting benches, working the transparency projector, or greeting visitors. I promised to be open to His leading and to say yes when asked, and that is what I did.

I remembered the story of my pastor sharing a similar attitude to finding his purpose. He also started by experimenting with various roles until he found his calling. All I did was to apply the principle in my own way and kept at it. An additional benefit I have found with this approach is that each role taught me skills which are now being used to enhance the ministry and work life today.

There is much work to do and numerous opportunities to serve others; use them to reveal your gifts, talents, develop skills and identify your purpose. If you are unemployed and seeking a job, you should volunteer at the place you aspire to find employment or where you can develop that well-needed experience employers are seeking. Therefore, when any vacancy occurs, you will have the competencies needed as well.

David was a son who had a great calling upon his life in the area of governmental leadership. Before he got there, he was trained to lead animals (as a shepherd), which meant he would have both soft skills and leadership skills necessary for his real purpose. In that job, David had to fight off bears and lions, resulting in the development of his defensive skills and leading him to become a protector of those under his care. It was those experiences serving helpless sheep that built him the faith to kill Goliath (the giant), propelling his real purpose and success, that of becoming king.

David played many menial roles before he walked into the purpose for which God created him. He did not rise to purpose overnight, but did his best with every task given, learning from the lessons, and growing. When the opportunity came, he had the charisma, soft skills, and other qualities needed for him to be the type of leader he became. These obstacles David faced made him recognize his strengths and weaknesses, but more importantly, the role of God in his life and the empowerment he received to do anything. David even played the role of a delivery man, which catapulted him to being at the right place at the right time. Allow no one to look down on your task or job and make you feel inferior. David's attitude was one of humility, so once sent by his father to his brothers who were on the battlefield, he went willingly.

There are too many people want to be king, who want to get there without the necessary qualifications. Clearly, it does not only mean a degree when I refer to qualifications. It means too many persons want to ascend to leadership positions before building up themselves, or garnering skills through their acts of service, and without updating those resumes.

When it was David's turn, he knew, because he had been through enough to know that he was able to take on this massive task before him. While he was in his waiting period after being anointed by Samuel, the priest, he kept doing small tasks and taking them seriously. It was through those situations, that His knowledge about God grew and his faith was anchored in Him. David was not terrified or daunted by the voice of the haters, whether it was his brothers or Goliath. He was ready, so he stepped out and rescued the nation, winning the favour of the people and the outgoing king. Choose to serve which will develop skills that will assist you when you are to move into your 'Promised land," that is, your designated purpose and success.

Revelation and Insight through Consultation

Another approach I took was to gain revelation and insight through consultation. I asked my friends, disciplers and mentor to share what they believe I am called to do and what were my gifts. I was, and still am still convinced that 1 Corinthians 12 is true. Each person has been given at least one gift. My friends and mentor shared the gifts they recognized in me, which was helpful information. For many years, I questioned their views, mainly because it did not line up with my personal preference. I wanted to do other things and preferred other spiritual gifts. But the different experiences garnered have proved them true. The spiritual gifts they identified, along with others He has given me, make up the list of gifts from which I now operate. This approach requires keeping an open mind as you receive the feedback.

During a discussion recorded in Mathew 16:20 between Jesus and his disciples, He asked, "Who do people say that the Son of Man is?" Later, he asked them, "Who do you say I am?" This, of course, was not because Jesus was having an identity crisis. He was getting a feel for people's views of Him, which would be based on how they had experienced Him. Then He asked those closest to Him their opinion. There is no need to be afraid to ask others about their opinions in this regard. Their responses will have to be examined, before being accepted.

Ask the people who are closest to you, the brave truth speakers, who will tell you not what you prefer to hear but the truth, about your calling and capabilities. As you work and relate to others, they will see you from a different perspective and may also recognize things about you that you did not know about yourself. It is that additional perspective that you need knowledge of to confirm or redefine your thoughts bring a more rounded understanding of who you are, how you are and what you possess. For example, in teacher training institutions, to help student-teachers determine the areas for improvement and to identify their strengths as they pursue this profession, the supervising lecturers evaluate several teaching episodes. Then they would provide feedback on the aspiring teachers' progress. It may even help student-teachers determine if they needed to reconsider their pursuit. Their birds-eye view serves to track progress, which proves helpful as the student-teacher sorts through the confusion with which many enter the institution. This legitimizes my recommendation, as asking others who have been around you for a long period would have the best insight on the matter.

Over the years, I have met many people who believed their calling was in a particular field of employment but did not demonstrate possession of the aptitude required for that profession. I remember when I taught at the high school level it was time to have students choose subjects that corresponded with their desired occupation. Year after year, we would see students failing miserably in a particular area of study, for example, all three Science subjects. Their results should have guided their choices, as they were not displaying the propensity to succeed in this field, but many would opt to register for the Science courses. It was a case of them choosing an area based on prestige, parents' choice, or childhood dream, but not based on facts. As teachers, we would have to redirect students based on their strengths, helping parents to see that success is not limited to one career. Once this was done, the students usually excelled.

Ask yourself the reason behind the choices you are making, and the motives will provide insight. We should trust others' opinions as we pray, as they may be able to confirm if our perceived calling, desired job, and partner line up with our gifts, persona, and competencies. With their special seat in our lives, they should be able to shed some light on the matter.

My Journal: Points to Remember

Which of these approaches do I need to adopt? How will I use this information to change how I approach finding my purpose? What is your take-away?

Breaking the Mindset

Mindsets are thought patterns that govern our lives, how we process information, deal with problems, and what we declare from our lips. It is a thought process inculcated over time from our experiences, through culture, education, family background, religious exposure, and friendships. The mind is the central processing unit of the body. It dictates how we function. The battlefield of the mind is a serious war that must be won.

Today, many people disregard the need to feed the mind as we take pains to feed the body, leaving some people mentally mal-nourished. This has led to a paucity of thoughts, and the processing system mal-functions easily. It results in mistrust, fear, doubt, lack of confidence, inability to connect with others, and engagement in activities that are destructive.

At some point, we should perform an analysis as to where we are and the reason for our state of affairs, to determine the type of mindset we have and its health level. If no stock is taken, then no matter the truth around us, we will never be able to accept it and truly achieve our full potential. There needs to be a turnaround point, and that starts here, recognizing our mindset and its hindrances.

A mindset check is necessary if you ever find yourself asking, "Why does this always happen to me?" Our mindset is like a broken record. Even if it is not working, there is a sense that I cannot break free from it. The good news is that you can be free from a faulty mindset by the power of God Almighty. In His years of ministry, Jesus declared many people free. He also told His disciples they would do greater things than He did. He brought release to the mindsets held by religious people, the sick, the mourners, sinners at the temple court, fishermen who were unlearned and disregarded, and many others. Jesus can do the same for us. If you find yourself framing or blaming others for the results you are facing constantly, then there is a mindset that needs to be broken and mended by the power of the Holy Spirit and the word of God.

A mindset exposes us to strongholds being fortified in our lives. Have you ever come across people who are sick and will engage in many different types of activities to gain healing, except asking the elders of the church to pray for them? They never seem to grasp the concept that God is All-powerful and, as Creator, can restore health by rebalancing the mind and body. Persons who are at this place have a stronghold. But the scripture in 2 Corinthians 10:5 makes it clear that believers possess the power to pull down strongholds and every high thing that sets itself up above the knowledge of God. Knowledge has to do with the mind.

Some people are now at the place of knowing their purpose, while others are at the place of implementing the strategies explained in the previous chapter. However, walking into purpose necessitates a shift in mindset away from doubt and fear, guilt and shame, and low self-confidence.

Realizing your purpose is one thing but walking into it is very important. There are people I know who have received direct prophetic words as well as clear direction as to the call of God on their lives, yet still, walk around aimlessly asking for more confirmation. What they really need is to cross the hurdle of mindset. They are held back because they cannot believe the word. The mind has somehow distorted the reality of the call rendering them stagnant, while others wait for the activation of the gifts they have been given.

Individuals ought to get to a place, no matter where in the process they are, to start reprogramming their minds to accept the purpose of their existence. Romans 12 urges us to renew our minds so we can walk in the good, pleasing, and perfect will of God. Paul called us to think about ourselves with sober judgement, not more highly than we ought, which means not lower than we are either. Whatever we are called to do, we should just do it.

The Holy Spirit empowers believers to work for the Lord in their field of employment, ministry, and in whatever state they find themselves. It is possible to overcome oneself and walk in freedom from these obstacles of the mind. Let us examine how to overcome these self-hurdles.

Mindset of Fear and Doubt

Fear and doubt are serious obstructions to success and living out your purpose. Fear is the feeling that the unknown should be dreaded. While doubt is a sense of uncertainty stemming from not being sure things are possible. These "twins" hold us back from progressing.

After Adam and Eve committed the sin of disobedience, the next thing that happened was that they became afraid, resulting in them hiding from the Lord. This account shows where fear stepped into our existence. Fear came about after sin and because its roots is from a sinful act, therefore it cannot be good.

Fear and doubt can influence you to the point where you neither go up or down, right, or left, but remain stationary. These are shackles that prevent people from walking into their purpose. It is a mental state that needs to be disarmed for progress to be made. When Elijah became fearful of Queen Jezebel, it put his life into a tailspin, which made him run away from his assignment. These twin sisters have put great men and women out of place, and off course. In fact, in the scriptures, variations of the phrase "fear not" can be found over 350 times. Clearly, while this emotion is a natural response, it is a state of mind that should be temporary.

There was a time in my life when these two hurdles kept me safely away from walking in purpose. If asked to read publicly I would shake like a leaf being harassed by the wind. I was fearful of being judged. The thought of making mistakes, standing before an audience, and walking towards the pulpit would be my downfall, so I avoided taking my place in the Kingdom. Fear and doubt crippled me to the point where I had to be delivered. I also had to break their power by studying and meditating on the word of God concerning me, which created a mind reset with its truth.

Therefore, a change of mindset through exposing yourself to truthful, positive materials and self-talk that has truth embedded so it can be implanted into your psyche is necessary. What you believe will dictate the level at which you can operate. Be deliberate in sourcing information that will challenge your thoughts and meditate on it. This state of being is not to be entertained, but to be removed.

It also involves jumping off and believing you will stand. I had to accept an assignment that forced me to face my fear, dispelling the mindset I possessed. The second book of Timothy 1:7 reveals that while there were many gifts given to the church, fear was not one of them.

If there is any intention to overcome or reject fear and doubt requires the identification of the strengths you possess, a determination to just do it and an acknowledgement of how far you have come. Many people I know have dreams but postpone them until retirement because they do not believe they could be successful now. Heresy! With the right mind-set, you can accomplish your dream before you are too old to appreciate it.

Mindset of Guilt and Shame

Mindsets are hard to break or change, especially when they are embedded in the past. Guilt and shame are the consequence of feeling remorse for an action, speech, or thought. It stems from a lack of self-forgiveness, where you believe what you did was so bad you do not deserve to be forgiven and let go. This is not necessarily linked to how others treat you, but how you perceive how you would treat others. Being released from guilt and shame is not easy, but possible. Both will certainly hinder you from taking hold of your purpose.

Being free from self-condemnation because you are worth it must be the new mindset. That which has already happened should not be a shackle. Confessing past actions and deciding to handle similar situations better should be the goal. It is about demonstrating that you have benefitted from the negative experience, especially in the case where you are attempting to rebuild trust within a relationship.

It is also important never to lose sight of the accuser. According to Scripture, his intention is to steal, kill, and destroy. Becoming trapped in a mindset of guilt can cause an abortion of one's purpose. Therefore, reaching a place of accepting forgiveness is golden.

For some people, guilt stems from not stepping up and doing what they feel convinced they should be doing. While for others, guilt stems from being taken advantage of and thinking they should have known better.

Some have stayed in jobs where they no longer feel fulfilled in order to fulfil family obligations, or for financial reasons, or to live up to the expectations of others, and to keep up appearances. They remain out of purpose and further away from success. Ultimately, they are out of the will of God.

Not exercising our faith keeps us bound. He who calls you will keep you and that which has been committed to Him. Guilt tends to lead to shame.

Struggling with shame becomes the lens through which everything is seen. Forgiving yourself is the greatest obstacle to moving past your past. Accepting our humanity, prone to having fallen short in life, releases us from guilt. Unforgiveness is a sign of pride and comes most of the time from a spirit of condemnation. Giving yourself a break causes a release from shame. Jesus did not come to bring condemnation, but freedom. No matter the reason for your guilt and shame, you can be free. Ultimately, appealing to God for forgiveness and knowing He accepts you even when you fall short. If God no longer holds it against you, then who are you to hold it against yourself? Additionally, ask God to give you the strength to forgive yourself and then let go. Focus on the new opportunities that are created so you can step out in purpose.

Lack of Self-Confidence

This is a serious trouble spot for many persons. They will refuse to get involve or step out and will often explain they are shy. Philippians 4:13 states, "I can do all things through Christ who strengthens me." This verse is my childhood mantra, which increased my self-confidence. It still challenges my own inhibitions and speaks to my reliance, my source. Attempting great things for God comes by faith. Knowing that I have God with me to supply my needs, to strengthen and direct my path, and to protect me from danger, helps to keep me grounded. If I rely on my own ability, my confidence would waiver, so I do not. It is important to keep things in proper perspective, to ensure you soar to new heights. My limitations do not stop God from picking up where I lack the faith to do.

Walking into one's purpose will be impeded if you do not have a proper view of who you are and your worth. Many people wait for others to build them up and so never get to the next level. Instead, they are stuck because they cannot find it within themselves to step out of the boat. There is no confidence in their ability and none in God's plan, so they never experience the length of their wings. The record reveals that when King David found himself discouraged, abandoned, and in a place where no encouragement was forthcoming, he stopped and spoke to himself. He brought himself to take account of what could have caused the feeling of discouragement, then directed himself to trust in the Lord. He called upon himself to reflect on his situation and commanded himself to believe it.

Believing in yourself will force others to believe in you. It is like entering a yard with a ferocious dog. If you give off fear, he picks up the scent and chases after you. But if you step in fearlessly, he cringes in the corner, making it possible for you to carry out your business without any hindrances. Going for that job interview, seeking to be joined in holy matrimony, or accepting that new ministry call, on your life is not easy, and it is often impossible with self-doubt. But, if you put your faith in the right person, then there will be no stopping you.

While many argue that confidence is built on the words of others only, it must be made clear that it is built more on your words, or your acceptance of words spoken concerning your life. We must decide what we will accept and what we will hold on to as our mantra. Joshua declared that he and his family had made a resolution to serve the Lord no matter what came their way. He made that his determination in the face of hardship through his declaration. It is important to echo the following words in challenging times: "I will believe, no matter where I find myself. I will believe it, and no matter what others choose, I will hold on."

Failure Mindset

The Word of God shares the stories of human failure from the first book to the end. Two stories of failure include those of Peter's failure to stand up for Jesus and Judas' failure to remain committed to Jesus. At the end of the events, they were both faced with the reality of the results of their personal failures and had to decide how to proceed. They could choose to stay in the pit or press forward to overcome it. Some people would get stuck there like Judas and take their lives. This taking of life entails not only the physical absence of life, but also being buried by failure-related thoughts.

Now despite Peter's failures to keep his temper in check, resisting the urge to remove the ear from the solider, his rebuke of Jesus' words, and ultimate denial, he decided to keep going after repentance in tears. He had a long line of failures, which could have crippled him and made him think he would always be a failure. He had to put off the failure mindset of condemnation and refocus on the course charted for him.

After Jesus' ascension, Peter stepped up to preach and lead the body of Christ during one of the hardest times in the history of the church. If failure has held you back from progressing to follow the path you are being led to pursue, then it is time to shake that off and refocus. Always keep in mind that failure is a part of life. The only One who is perfect is God Almighty.

Sometimes we digress when confronted with failure, but we must speak to our failures, and then bring closure to the mindset. People are made to rise, not to succumb to failure, which means the Designer, God, knew failure was going to come, but He had also provided a way out of sinking. It is for each person to accept that failure is not the end of their life, but a new phase, perhaps, or an opportunity to arise.

My Journal: Points to Remember

With what mindset (s) are you struggling and how will you change that? What is your take-away?

Traps Affecting the Assignment

Paul, the Apostle, penned that the things he wanted to do, he was not doing but things he did not want to do that is what he found himself doing (Romans 7:15). It affected the assignment that was on his life, which I can relate to. The assignment on your life is not going to happen without effort. There are going to be pitfalls that hinder your progress, and these must be addressed to ensure you possess the land. When Abraham left home for the Promised Land, all he had was a command to go. He went obediently, paying close attention to the word of direction until he arrived, and Lot, his nephew, became his "trap". Conflict arose between Abraham and Lot's men, which could have derailed the purpose of God in Abraham's life. So, Uncle Abraham had allowed Lot to go his own way on his preferred terms, to ensure he stay in purpose.

There are times when we try to be in purpose and take others on the journey with us. However, instead of aiding the assignment, they become a hinderance to it. We must be prepared when we recognize the trap to escape it by separating ourselves from them.

These external traps are designed to keep people out of their purpose. Therefore, while the decision may be hard, it is the only way to ensure one's future is not ruined. Other external forces include the pronouncements of others over your life. There are deliberate traps to disrupt God's plan for you and fosters an environment that brings opposition.

Others' Pronouncements Trap

The pronouncements of others can have a serious impact on your assignment. When Moses was getting ready to lead the people of Israel into the land of Canaan, ten spies said, the assignment was impossible. They spoke defeat about the purpose for which Moses was called, to lead the people back to the land promised to them by God. He had to decide on whose report he would believe, the ten negative voices or the two who encouraged him to hold on to the word of the Lord for his mission. Because of his relationship with God, Moses chooses to hold on to the word he originally received.

Have you ever noticed that the minority group is the one who believes in your purpose? Perhaps that should be a tester. Is everyone in agreement with your decision? Then it might not be the right one. When Jesus expressed that his purpose was coming into being, most of the disciples objected, even though they had been with him for three years and heard him identify it as the reason He came.

You must seriously consider who is speaking into your ear, as they control your reach. The job you apply for is possible. The business you want to start is not bigger than you. The desire to travel is not only for the affluent, as many will want you to believe. Find those who will celebrate your success and keep them around you. Not everyone wants to see you succeed, so figure out who is genuinely there in good times and difficult times. Then you will be able to trust the words spoken over you.

Blockage Traps

Some people choose to deliberately put stumbling blocks in your way to hamper your purpose. The story of Nehemiah is one good example. He returned home to restore the wall of his country, not for fame or glory, but to honor God. On his arrival, he prayed for three days, did undercover work to assess what was to be done, and then divulged his purpose to the people. While on the job, two men, Sanballat and Tobiah, decided they were going to stop his plans (Neh. 4). This is nothing new, I am sure you have your own story of people trying to distract you from accomplishing your goals or completing your course. There may have also been times when they try to prevent you from applying for the job or promotion, making the bid to acquire property a challenge, or hijacking the project you were assigned by your superior.

These men made many attempts to stop the project. They made false accusations about Nehemiah's intentions. They questioned his motives, and reporting this to the leadership to get him in trouble. Nehemiah, on the other hand, kept on praying, continued the work, and never came down to meet with them. He never stopped to clarify the issues or contended with them or sort out the lies. He just motivated the others and never stopped.

When you are on your way to progress, not every meeting should be attended, and not every accusation should be argued. We should know some of these things are just to derail us. Nehemiah knew he was walking in purpose, so he refused to be distracted by them and kept on task. These two men went as far as to threaten his life. It got so intense that even the workers supporting Nehemiah had to be armed while working because of their threats, as they decided there was no turning back. He went full speed ahead and saw the completion of the wall.

The lesson, I believe, is clear: to fly the trap of the detractors means ignoring their distractions and keeping working on yourself and your goals while putting things in place to alleviate the impact of their deeds. He shared the situation with his vision carriers, so they knew how to respond in case the walls were breached. He anticipated potential problems and put safeguards in place to deal with them.

Removing a blockage trap requires analysis of the situation, planning for eventualities, and keep working to carry out your purpose. Many times, we are trapped and remain that way because we do not share with our destiny helpers the challenges, preparing them to stand with us despite the negative atmosphere and lies.

Another noticeable approach applied by Nehemiah was to stay in the presence of God. He maintained constant and consistent prayer sessions. He understood for his success to be realized he needed to remain in contact with the only One who knows the future and has the ability to fly every trap possible. The importance of building one's relationship as you go cannot be overstated, for He will lead and direct us in the way we should go.

Environmental Traps

At times, the environment you find yourself in may go counter to the purpose for which you were designed. By this, I may mean socioeconomic situations, past experiences, physical limitations, family life and even the weather. While these are not new traps, they can significantly affect your destiny. It is not always possible to move to a new location, however, there are ways to thrive and excel right there where you are planted in that season.

There are numerous real-life experiences recorded where the environment posed a problem for the person trying to walk into purpose. For example, when Moses faced the Red Sea, Joshua the River Jordan, and when Jesus enabled Peter to walk on water. There were also the times when Jesus allowed the disciples to participate in the miraculous feeding of the over 5000 who were hungry but were not able to get food. The paralyzed man at the pool of Bethesda, and the widow of Zarephath are additional evidence. Each faced environmental traps but got help and overcame them. Examination of this trap revealed that help is needed, as some of the issues are bigger than our capabilities.

There are some circumstances that no one can help you out of; it's just you and God. For these situations, only Supernatural intervention can change things. In the examples cited above the hand of God enabled the transition.

To be free also required obedience to the directions of God. Moses had to step up and raise his hands for the sea to part. Joshua had the priest take the ark and stand in the water, and it stood on two sides. Then, Peter had to step out on Jesus' words to walk on water, and the disciples had to locate the five loaves and two fish. The paralyzed man had to rise for his healing, and the widow had to make the cake for the prophet to walk into overflow.

Faith is the other ingredient to escaping the environmental traps blocking your assignment. These obedient acts were faith in operation. Many of us have not seen our environment change because we misunderstand the amount of faith needed. It is not a mountain portion that is required, just a mustard seed amount, and things would be different. Once you practice listening to Jesus during prayer, His voice becomes familiar enabling you to distinguish between your thoughts and God's leading removing any uncertainty and allow you to walk with purpose.

My Journal: Points to Remember

In what traps are you being ensnared? What will you do to break free? What is your take-away?

The God-Directed Life

In this twenty-first century, where many have chosen to be led by feelings, we have seen an increase in alternative family and lifestyles, school shootings, the use of media for wealth, and callous attitudes of children towards taking care of their parents. The Bible sums it up in three temptations: the lust of the flesh, the lust of the eyes, and the pride of life (1 John 2:16). The flesh is physical pleasure, the eyes are to covet or materialism, and pride is the desire for power and recognition. These three have engulfed many, leading them away from living the submitted life. People are focused on meeting their needs and having fun, to the neglect of others. I remember being taught at church that there is a choice in who directs your life; I could either with my limited knowledge, or I could allow God, who is omniscient, to direct my life. It is important to make that decision upfront and not just saunter through life in the middle. On this issue, there is no compromise.

In every kingdom, there is a codebook with the protocols, norms, and expectations for citizens. The Bible is the Christian's guidebook as to how the King of kings expects us to operate. It also tells us how to succeed by walking in obedience and fulfilling our God-intended purpose. Therefore, once you are a believer the word of God cannot be conditionally or occasionally read. King David said he stored the word in his heart so he would be guided by it and not violate God's precepts. He went further than reading it, to meditating on it and memorizing it. There is great value in knowing the Word, which is the sword of the

Spirit. It is what the Holy Spirit will use when challenges arise to equip us to function and encourage our faith to rise.

The Self-Directed Life

This is a life whose course is being chartered by the person, with no input from its Designer. It is when a person sits on the throne of their heart and determine what to do based on personal interest and desire. It is trusting in your limited knowledge and perceptions. The story of Achan (which in Hebrews means trouble) in the Bible reveals what happens to the life of someone who chooses to follow his own desires, taking some things God has instructed them not to take as plunder. His decision cost the Israelites dearly (Joshua 7). When someone decides to live solely for himself or herself it will negatively affect their success and make it difficult to live out their purpose.

The self-directed life is like what the judge would say to someone who wants to represent themselves in court; it is like having a fool for a lawyer. You have no one with the expertise to stand up for you when you need guidance or representation. It is the same thing in the parable of the Prodigal Son, who decided he wanted to govern his life, leaving his wise old father's home. When the harsh reality of life hit, he was alone (friends and family less), broke and hit rock bottom. Failure may not be immediate, but it will come.

The God Directed Life

If you allow God to take control. He is given permission to sit on the throne of your heart, directing your desires and steps. Being led is about having a relationship with God through Jesus Christ, who has plans to prosper, not to harm, giving hope and a future. I believe we must choose to invest in a policy with terms set to help, not harm, where the fine prints are written for our good. The God-directed person has the Ever-present, All-knowing, and All-wise God on their side. The one who holds the future is walking beside you. This is definitely a win-win situation as He is just a prayer away.

There is no need to fear the decisions you make once you are being guided by Him.

A God-centered life does not mean the absence of trouble, but the provision of safety and guidance. The Apostle Paul, after his conversion to Christianity, lived a God-centered life. He ended up writing most of the New Testament and starting many churches. When his days of trials came, even before his shipwreck took place, God revealed what would happen and enlightened him on how to respond. He was able to comfort the others and lead the entire fleet to safety, even though the ship was destroyed.

When I was in my early twenties, after seeking the Lord for direction for my life, He gave me the name of an institution of learning to attend. I was not aware the named institution existed, so I did some investigation at the church and was informed it did exist. I decided to follow the word to see where it would lead. I had hoped I would go to college one day but thought that was far from my grasp based on my family's financial state. After applying, attending the interview, and being accepted, I realized I could not afford the tuition. I was confident, however, it would be covered, so I accepted the opportunity to attend. God never failed to take care of me for the four years I attended. I knew that once He is in charge, everything would work out in my favor, and it did. Being directed has certain guarantees. For example, you will never be abandoned as God promises never to leave us nor forsake us, in good times or bad (Hebrews 13:5).

To live a God-directed life is to exhibit a willingness to submit our wills to God's leading. Unlike what some may believe, submitting is not a sign of weakness, but a sign of strength. It is surrendering your desires and interests to God by faith.

Giving God charge does not abdicate our responsibility, but it brings peace of mind. You may be experiencing mental turmoil, anxiety, situational issues, or crippling circumstances that you cannot see your way out of. Turning your life over to God will certainly make it better. He promised to raise you up like an eagle, so that you would run and not get tired and walk without faint (Isaiah 40:31). His Word will guide how you live, while prayer provides a way for you to share your concerns with Him. You will not live this life alone. There is a group of witnesses on the same path you have chosen, some ahead of you on the journey or in a similar place as you, on whom you can also rely for guidance.

When you decide to live the God-directed life, you receive the gift of the Holy Spirit. His job is to dwell inside you, providing the guidance that you need. He allows you to hear heaven's direction for your life, so you walk in God's master plan. He is known as the Comforter, who will give peace in times of trouble. The Holy Spirit is also the Revelator of truth, which means He will help you discern what God's will for your life is. In fact, He is present to bring to memory all the Lord has spoken to us. It means that when you are confronted with speaking on a matter, He will guide your speech, enabling you to answer appropriately even during an interview.

Now, the Holy Spirit will give us directions, but we must be prepared to listen. Many people will confess that if they had listened, following the leading of the Holy Spirit, things would have gone much differently. He cannot be held accountable for our decision to ignore His leading. He is the same quality as Jesus, and therefore is omniscient, which means He knows everything. Whom do you choose to rely on? Is it you, with your limited knowledge, or He, who holds the future?

Many people spend much time praying and fasting, which are important spiritual disciplines, but miss a key ingredient. They fail to listen to the response. They just want to ensure He was told about the matter, so we absolve ourselves of taking responsibility for the outcome. This cannot be the way of the God-directed life. Direction means following what is required, yet we want to stay at the helm, allowing God to intervene when we are in tight spots but holding Him at bay when things are going well.

When Moses went before the Lord on many occasions in the book of Exodus, he explained the situation they faced but waited for a word from the Lord to determine how to proceed. Unless the Lord spoke, Moses would remain in His presence no matter how long it took. In today's fast-paced society, we just want to drop (pray) and roll (go). But God wants to be a part of our lives. From creation, it is evident that God wants to have a personal relationship with mankind, His creation. Through the Angel Gabriel and Paul's dreams, he spoke to Cain, Noah, Abraham, Mary, and Zachariah. He is still interested in speaking to humans, so ensure you give Him the opportunity and build that relationship with Him.

Guiding Principles

Listening for His voice is one way to know if God is leading you to do or to be something. The more you commune with someone, the easier voice recognition becomes. Rather than getting confused about whether it is our minds or Him, we should check it against the biblical teachings to ensure that what is heard does not going against it. The word lining up and not contradicting the Scripture is a good indicator that it is from the Lord Jesus Christ.

The second checkpoint is to see if it conveys the peace that surpasses all understanding. If it does, it is most likely from Him. This is not to say all the words God will give will be easy to follow, but knowing they are His words will bring peace to one's soul and mind, which under normal conditions would be troubling.

Thirdly, listen keenly to the words spoken by God's servants (prophet or preachers) as they share. From my experience over the years, God does not speak only once or through one method. Usually, you will hear the same or similar sentiments being shared by others. Your peers could also be used to confirm the word you are unsure about.

My Journal: Points to Remember

What is preventing you from living a God-directed life, and how will you overcome it? What is your take-away?

The Keys to Bursting Forth

A few years ago, my husband, who does a little home gardening, planted some corn. Several of them started to burst forth from the ground, but there were a few that did not. He started to look closer at each hole where they were planted, and he noticed one under a small stone. It was bent over and seemingly struggling to become a corn stalk that bore fruit. He decided to remove the obstacle so that the young shoot could reach its potential. Sometime after, he visited the garden and noticed the transformation of that very plant. Life is like that for many of us. There is so much potential for us to grow and develop, but we need to have something removed for us to blossom and bloom. It is never too late to succeed in life. Whether it is success in marriage, job promotion, business, ministry or whatever you desire, there is no time limit. It is possible!

Over 10 years ago, the Lord laid it on my heart to host a weekend conference for the wives of ministers in the Kingdom. I tried to get partnerships from friends who are wives of ministers. While the support was expressed, it was to no avail. I carried that vision and prayed many prayers of apology to God for not walking out by faith. At one point, I hoped God would lift the sensing, but it never went away. When I preach, I would refer to aspects of it without supplying the details.

Then one early morning in January 2021 I heard God's voice instructing me to host the conference in March 2021 virtually. I decided to follow the leading of the Lord, and I burst forth. The sense of that came with walking in obedience and starting a ministry is unexplainable. Oh yes, a ministry. He gave me the named First Lady International. The goal is to offer C.A.R.E., that is, Connection, Activation, Refreshment and Empowerment, to wives of minister who operate in the Fivefold Ministry. A God-inspired ministry was born. Since then, the vision has been growing. I am realizing that when God gives a vision, it includes progressive revelations. Do not let delays of any kind make you feel you should abandon God's mission or ministry in your life.

Everyone is created to fulfill a purpose, something unique to them. To do so, the lid must be removed, whether it be placed by others, our minds, or the enemy of our soul. Bursting forth required the plant to push against the stone that barred its entry into the world. If not, it would have been underground and then died.

You must determine in your mind that you will no longer remain underground; you will push against the barriers so you can be seen, and help can come to you. The story of David, the shepherd boy, has a similar theme. A young boy was sent to the battle to do a menial task. Not even his own father thought he could do more than take care of the sheep and serve his brothers. He was buried for years. In fact, he was so buried that when the prophet Samuel came to anoint the future king of Israel, his father did not call him to the line-up. The prophet had to ask if there was no other son because he was convinced the Lord had said one of Jesse's sons would take over from Saul. It was sometime later that Jesse mentioned he had a young son, but with much doubt. It took the Spirit of God to identify him, or he would have been overlooked.

David was not allowed to enlist in the army, to offer himself for the battle. Sometime later, he was sent to bring food supplies for his brother on the battlefield. While there, David snatched the opportunity to push against the limitations of age, inexperience, and others' unbelief in his ability. He volunteered to fight the giant, Goliath, who had taunted his countrymen for days. No one would have asked him to fight just by looking at him, so he created his own opportunity through his speech. He spoke loudly enough and to the right people who could get him to the next level by sharing his faith and vision. David found his destiny connector who got him into a dialogue with King Saul. This was not without his brothers, who tried to keep him buried by accusing him of unfaithfulness to their father's flock, being inquisitive and insensitive enough to enquire about Goliath. However, David pushed past the negative comments and declared his faith and interest in serving God at any cost. He stepped out of his "hiding place" and was seen by the one who overheard his faith words. Then the king "removed the stone" so David could rise and fight, bringing victory to the Israelites. This shift was not just for this moment but created a future shift for him to attain his divine purpose.

Living in time has caused us as people to assign time to everything, and when these are not met, we give up and walk in failure. By now, you must recognize that this does not have to be your reality. David did not use his age or lack of military experience to keep him under a lid, and neither should we. The key David used was his past experiences, knowledge of his God and actively pursuing his goal. There are experiences we have had that were orchestrated to teach us lessons for life. For some, they have been used to keep us imprisoned, while for others, they are used as scaffolds to go higher and soar. Past experiences, no matter the intention of the participants, should be reviewed and lessons used to fuel our path.

The other key David used was his knowledge of how God operates and his limitlessness. He used that to fuel his thoughts and perception of the situation. When everyone around him was in fear because they saw the size of the giant, he saw the power of his God. He used kingdom principles to guide him in what he invested his time in. David could have joined in the conversation and shared his opinion, then left, as he was free to do so. However, he reviewed the situation and believed God would fight for them. Promotion does not come from the east or west but from the Lord, so if you see a position, you are desirous of, do not shrink back from it because of small talkers or haters or the fearful.

The next key is to actively pursue your goal. Step out, that is, to push forward knowing that if it is in the will of the Lord, it shall be yours. Send that application, meet with that person, start that ministry, go to that place, establish that business, write that book, paint that artwork, or whatever it takes to ensure you are not denied. Make this your mantra: I refuse to be denied.

We must do our part in changing our set destiny to walk into divine destiny. Many times, our background, family history, and words spoken over us have kept us from bursting forth. However, David demonstrated the need to speak up when you get access to the 'playfield of advancement. Offering our services can open many doors that would have otherwise been closed to us. Even if you are not at the leadership level, speak by faith and the lid will be pushed away just enough for your connector to find you.

How can I burst forth?

Talking by faith will only come when you spend time with the Master Builder. To have the right perspective on a product usually requires information from the producer of that item. Human beings were created by God. Therefore, to fully understand and appreciate ourselves will require us to find out what He designed us for and how He sees us.

People need to know who we are and what purpose we were created for. This comes from daily reading the scripture and having the right perspective on our abilities, assets we have access to, and God's expectations for us so we can push against the grain. The Bible is the Word of God, which shares promises and His desires for humans (His master plan). A change of mindset is needed for people to push off the lid placed upon them. The book of Romans describes the need for the mind to be renewed.

Additionally, spending time in worship, prayer, and fasting will roll away the stone.

These moments with God must not be taken for granted because He will lead us into green pastures, as Psalm 23 says and prepared a feast in the presence of our enemies. Therefore, we can get clear insight once we spend the most precious commodity available to us, time.

Time is given to all. However, we get to decide how it is spent. You can go about trying to figure it out, or you can go before the Lord Jesus Christ in sincerity and have Him lead you to the right path. In His presence, stones are rolled away, for no one object or person can stop God's plan for your life. Our souls are watered in His presence, which will cause us to grow and flourish.

The world has so many hurting people who only spew their hurt towards the vulnerable. We cannot embrace hurtful words and remain buried. David's own brothers spoke ill of him in front of others; his response was to ignore them, then clarify where his help came from and to go straight to King Saul. He did not let that sink in; instead, he asked others to explain the situation they were in. We may have to leave the familiar people around to us inquire about how to change certain situations. It also helps is garner a fresh perspective from God.

To burst forth, you must be opened to dreaming. Dreams can be the catalyst for you to believe. Joseph was a dreamer. While it caused the relationship with his family to be shaky, he kept on believing and sharing. Joseph held on to what he saw, and years later, it all came to pass. A dream does not always happen after it is deposited in you, but the seed buried will grow. Allow yourself to catch a vision of God's purpose for you and then walk worthy so it will come to pass.

Recently, I was talking with a friend who shared something profound. My friend explained something she discovered about a word she received, and I will add that it can be applied to a dream. She shared that for the word to come to pass, we have a role to honour God. We no can longer just live as we please because the word should take over our lives. Once you have a dream, of course not necessarily of the nocturnal type, you should start conceptualizing how it can be realized. Thinking, crossing your fingers tightly and hoping will not do.

Preparation for success is the key to bursting forth. Take stock of where you are and what it will take to get you there. Then start working on it, little by little, or in chunks if possible. This implies that on the off chance you need to retool, learn new ideas, apparatus, how to converse with a companion, do interviews there is effort made to acquire them or sort through them.

Get ready by attending seminars or doing a short course to prepare yourself for when the opportunity arises. This will guarantee that when you hear the thump of opportunity in your entryway, you can meet it with excitement and not fear. The key is to apply yourself, using what you possess. You cannot pretend to be someone else or ignore your dream if you don't hold on to it. In fact, remind yourself of it and review plans regularly to identify where you are on the path to success. It was a. leap of faith, Burst Forth…Arise.!

My Journal: Points to Remember

What will you do to ensure you burst forth? What is your take-away?

ARISE BIBLICAL PRINCIPLES

The word Arise conveys the idea that a change of state or position is possible and perhaps necessary. It means someone is below where they could be and has the capacity to do something about it. Using these bible verses this verb will be discussed.

Genesis 35:3 *"And let us arise, and go up to Bethel; and I will make there an altar unto God, who answered me in the day of my distress, and was with me in the way which I went*". In order to succeed, you have to get up, wake up, change your position and change your location. Staying where we are at will only ensure we are stagnant and unfruitful. Moving from Aspiration Station and going to a place where you can receive an answer when you feel like giving up is necessary. This place is at the altar of the Lord. Build Him a space in your life.

Genesis 13:17 "*Arise, walk through the land in the length of it and in the breadth of it; for I will give it unto thee.*" This was the instruction given to Abram by the Lord. The Lord can open doors to prosperity in your life as well. The earth is the Lord's, so it is good to remember that at times we must walk through and take position.

Surveying the land before acquiring it is analogous to conducting research on the organization for which you wish to work so that when you go for the interview, you will be knowledgeable about the land. When we walk in obedience to God's direction, victory is secured, and that is what Abram did and received what was promised.

Isaiah 60:1 "*Arise, shine, for the light has come, and the glory of the Lord is risen upon you,*" speaks of the ability to stand because of the presence of the Almighty God in one's life. The glory of the Lord releases darkness from among His people. The enemy cannot stand against the presence of the Lord, so as you seek to step into purpose, do not fear the terror around or within. Cultivate your relationship with Jesus Christ of Nazareth.

Mark 2:11 *"I tell you, get up, take your mat and go home."* It conveys the message that each person needs to participate in the transformation of their state of being. While many things seek to keep us trapped and bound, with God's enabling, things can change. Therefore, I speak this verse to each reader, "Arise, take that which has made you comfortable and static. Step out!"

ABOUT THE AUTHOR

Andrea Richards is a committed Christian educator who has spent most of her life pouring into the lives of others. Presently, she is a Senior Lecturer at the Sam Sharpe Teachers' College situated in Western Jamaica and is pursuing a Doctor of Ministry in Christian Counselling at Andersonville Theological Seminary. Andrea holds qualification in the areas of Theology, Education, Guidance Counselling, Literacy and Shipping and Logistics Management. Andrea is a motivational speaker, a lay preacher, and a trained counsellor. She is the talk show host on the radio programme, Impactful Women aired on Impact Gospel Radio.

Andrea is the Founder and President of First Lady International, a ministry to the wives of Christian ministers that endeavors to form Connections, Activate, Refresh, and Empower those called to serve. Andrea and her husband, Rev. Lloyd Richards, are founders of the Links Mission Team, which seeks to impact lives with the Gospel and through practical ministries. She resides in Jamaica and is the mother of two children.

I am always willing to inspire others so for speaking engagement feel free to contact me.

Send Request to:
Facebook: @AndreaSRichardsAuthor
Email: Richards.andrea10@yahoo.com

For MORE Resources

- Get FREE eNewsletter
- Get EARLY Notice of Book Release
- Get FREE eJournal
- Mindset Checklist

REVIEW

Once you have read this book

please RATE and leave a **REVIEW**

on Amazon and my **Facebook Author's page!**

AUTHOR PAGE

@AndreaSRichardsAuthor *(Facebook)*

www.ingramcontent.com/pod-product-compliance
Lightning Source LLC
La Vergne TN
LVHW010452160826
845677LV00012B/2446

* 9 7 8 9 7 6 9 6 8 8 6 1 2 *